THE POETRY OF TELLURIUM

The Poetry of Tellurium

Walter the Educator

SKB

Silent King Books a WhichHead Imprint

Copyright © 2023 by Walter the Educator

All rights reserved. No part of this book may be reproduced in any manner whatsoever without written permission except in the case of brief quotations embodied in critical articles and reviews.

First Printing, 2023

Disclaimer
This book is a literary work; poems are not about specific persons, locations, situations, and/or circumstances unless mentioned in a historical context. This book is for entertainment and informational purposes only. The author and publisher offer this information without warranties expressed or implied. No matter the grounds, neither the author nor the publisher will be accountable for any losses, injuries, or other damages caused by the reader's use of this book. The use of this book acknowledges an understanding and acceptance of this disclaimer.

"Earning a degree in chemistry changed my life!"
- Walter the Educator

dedicated to all the chemistry lovers, like myself, across the world

CONTENTS

Dedication v

Why I Created This Book? 1
One - Tellurium, A Marvel Of Creation . . . 2
Two - Cosmic Affair 4
Three - Endless Delight 6
Four - Connection To The Universe 8
Five - Awe And Grace 10
Six - Genius Of Mankind 12
Seven - Technology's Song 14
Eight - Testament To Progress 16
Nine - Quest For Insight 18
Ten - Nature's Grandest Plan 20
Eleven - Life's Eternal Zest 22
Twelve - Guided By Tellurium 24

Thirteen - Universe Of Possibilities	. . . . . .	26
Fourteen - Forever Transforming	. . . . . .	28
Fifteen - Power Of Chemistry	. . . .	30
Sixteen - Symphony Of Elements	. . . . . .	32
Seventeen - Catalyst Of Our Dreams	. . . .	34
Eighteen - Endless Love	. . . .	36
Nineteen - Through The Darkest Night	. . . .	38
Twenty - World Of Innovation	. . . .	40
Twenty-One - Forever Sings	. . . .	42
Twenty-Two - Source Of Hope And Light	. .	44
Twenty-Three - A Future We Long To See	. .	46
Twenty-Four - Celestial Might	. . . .	48
Twenty-Five - Dear Element	. . . .	50
Twenty-Six - Tellurium, Our Ally	. . . .	52
Twenty-Seven - Pursuit Of Knowledge	. . . .	54
Twenty-Eight - Tellurium, Oh Tellurium	. . .	56
Twenty-Nine - Magical Force	. . . .	58
Thirty - Endless Praise	. . . .	60
Thirty-One - Work Of Art	. . . .	62
Thirty-Two - Bloom And To Flower	. . . . .	64

Thirty-Three - Poetic Muse	. . . .	66
Thirty-Four - Love And Care	. . . .	68
Thirty-Five - Precious Element	. . . .	70
Thirty-Six - Upon This Earth	. . . .	72
About The Author	. . . .	74

WHY I CREATED THIS BOOK?

Creating a poetry book about the chemical element Tellurium was an intriguing and unique endeavor. Tellurium, with its distinctive properties and symbolism, offers a rich source of inspiration. By exploring the various aspects of Tellurium, such as its atomic structure, historical significance, and cultural relevance, I can delve into themes of transformation, rarity, and the interconnectedness of the natural world. This allows for the creation of thought-provoking, imaginative, and evocative verses that bridge the scientific and artistic realms, offering readers a fresh perspective and a captivating reading experience.

ONE

TELLURIUM, A MARVEL OF CREATION

In secrets of the Earth's deep core,
A hidden jewel I do adore,
Born from stars, I proudly stand,
Tellurium, an element so grand.
    A lustrous metal, silvery-gray,
I dance with light, a radiant display,
In crystal form, my beauty gleams,
A celestial gem, beyond our dreams.
    In nature's realm, I'm seldom found,
Yet my allure knows no bound,
Beneath the ground, in rocks I reside,
A treasure sought by those who stride.

With atomic number fifty-two,
I'm known for my properties true,
A conductor, a semi-metal am I,
Electrons dancing, reaching the sky.

I whisper tales of ancient lore,
As alchemists sought me evermore,
Yet in their quest, they found me not,
For my essence, they could not unlock.

In modern times, I find a place,
In technology's swift-paced race,
In solar panels, I find my role,
Capturing sunlight, a source so whole.

From televisions to memory chips,
I bring innovation to our fingertips,
Tellurium, a marvel of creation,
Fueling progress, shaping our nation.

So, let us celebrate this element rare,
With wonder and awe, let us share,
For in its essence, we can find,
A glimpse of the universe, intertwined.

TWO

COSMIC AFFAIR

In the depths of the cosmos, a hidden jewel resides,
Born from the fiery hearts of stars, where creation collides.
Tellurium, a lustrous metal, so rare and so pure,
A dance with light, a treasure sought by those who endure.
A conductor of electricity, a semi-metal divine,
Tellurium weaves its magic, connecting the lines.
In the heart of technology, it finds its rightful place,
Powering solar panels, memory chips, a cosmic embrace.
Alchemists of old, their quest in vain,
To unlock its essence, forever they'd strain.
For Tellurium, a mystery, it chose not to unfold,
A secret held tightly, a story left untold.

Yet, in its shimmering presence, we catch a glimpse,
Of the universe intertwined, where wonder never dims.
Tellurium, a marvel of creation's design,
A glimpse into the cosmic, where worlds align.
   Oh Tellurium, you hold the key,
To progress and innovation, for all to see.
A silent guardian, a celestial guide,
In your atomic beauty, we find solace and pride.
   As we journey through time, seeking knowledge anew,
Tellurium, you remind us of the universe's view.
A jewel of the elements, so precious and rare,
Forever you'll shine, in the cosmic affair.

THREE

ENDLESS DELIGHT

In the depths of the universe, a jewel unseen,
A treasure born from the stars, Tellurium's gleam.
Lustrous metal it is, dancing with light,
A conductor of electricity, shining so bright.
　　Through the alchemists' quest, its essence they sought,
But the secrets it held, they never were caught.
A mystery it remained, for ages untold,
A story of wonder, as the centuries unfold.
　　Now it finds its purpose, in technology's hand,
Powering solar panels across the land.
Memory chips it engulfs, with knowledge it's filled,
A testament to its power, a promise fulfilled.
　　Oh Tellurium, rare and pure,
A cosmic connection, forever endure.

In progress and innovation, you play a role,
Unveiling the mysteries, that life may unfold.

A key to the knowledge, the universe's vast,
A reminder of wonders that forever will last.
Tellurium, oh element of grace and might,
In your presence, we find endless delight.

FOUR

CONNECTION TO THE UNIVERSE

In the depths of space, where stars doth gleam,
A cosmic dance, a celestial dream.
From fiery furnaces, a tale unfolds,
Of Tellurium, a treasure to behold.

Born from supernovas, in stellar embrace,
A lustrous metal, with ethereal grace.
Its atomic dance, a symphony of light,
Unveiling secrets, hidden in the night.

In alchemists' chambers, they sought to find,
The mystic power, Tellurium defined.
But their desperate hands, could not command,
The essence of this element, so grand.

Yet in the hands of science, it did find its way,
Unveiling wonders, in the light of day.

For in technology's realm, it found its worth,
Empowering progress, from its humble birth.

Solar panels bask, in its radiant glow,
Harnessing the sun's energy, as rivers flow.
Memory chips, with their intricate design,
Store our stories, for future minds to find.

Oh Tellurium, a cosmic gift so rare,
A bridge 'twixt heaven and earth, we share.
From distant galaxies, you've journeyed far,
To light our lives, like a guiding star.

So let us marvel, at your cosmic dance,
And honor your presence, with every chance.
For in your shimmering essence, we find,
A connection to the universe, so kind.

FIVE

AWE AND GRACE

In Tellurium's realm, a mystery unfolds,
A lustrous metal, with secrets untold.
Its atomic number, fifty-two it bears,
A cosmic element that silently shares.

Within the Earth's crust, it finds its place,
A rare treasure, a celestial embrace.
With a bluish-white hue, it gleams and shines,
A vision of beauty, a sight divine.

Tellurium, conductor of light,
In solar panels, you ignite,
Harnessing the sun's radiant power,
A symbol of progress, hour by hour.

Within memory chips, your presence resides,
Storing data, where innovation abides.
A testament to technology's might,
You pave the way for a future so bright.

O Tellurium, enigmatic and grand,
With your atomic weight, you command,
A cosmic dance, you partake,
Unveiling the universe, step by step, we make.

In laboratories, scientists explore,
Unraveling your secrets, forevermore.
A catalyst for progress, a key to the unknown,
Tellurium, your power, forever shown.

So, let us celebrate this element rare,
A symbol of wonder, beyond compare.
In science and technology's embrace,
Tellurium, you leave us in awe and grace.

SIX

GENIUS OF MANKIND

In the realm of elements, behold Tellurium,
A metalloid of lustrous, silvery sheen.
Its atomic number, fifty-two, a symphony,
Crafted by nature's ingenious machinery.
    A cosmic connection, Tellurium does possess,
Born from the fiery depths of Earth's caress.
Within its core, secrets it does store,
Unraveling mysteries, forevermore.
    In the realm of technology, Tellurium shines,
Harnessing the sun's energy, it aligns.
Solar panels, gleaming with a radiant hue,
Capturing sunlight, turning it into something new.
    Memory chips, a testament to its might,
Storing information, memories taking flight.

In the depths of circuitry, it weaves its spell,
Transforming data, the stories it tells.
A catalyst for progress, innovation's guide,
Tellurium, a companion by our side.
Scientific exploration, it propels us far,
Unveiling the secrets of distant stars.
Tellurium, an element of endless worth,
A bridge between heaven and Earth.
Its properties, a marvel to behold,
A testament to nature's story, so bold.
In the realm of elements, behold Tellurium,
A metalloid of wonder, forever in bloom.
Its legacy, etched in science's grand design,
A testament to the genius of mankind.

SEVEN

TECHNOLOGY'S SONG

In the realm of technology's dawn,
Where innovation is reborn,
A metalloid of rare allure,
Tellurium, we shall explore.

In solar panels, it finds its might,
Harnessing the sun's radiant light,
A shimmering bridge, a cosmic bond,
Transforming photons to electrons, beyond.

Memory chips, its memory's grace,
A matrix of bits, a digital embrace,
Storing data, a binary dance,
Tellurium, the conductor of chance.

A catalyst in chemical streams,
Unleashing reactions, fulfilling dreams,

Its presence felt in every stride,
Advancing progress, side by side.

Tellurium, a wondrous blend,
Of heaven's touch and Earth's descend,
A bridge between the two domains,
Where science and wonder intertwine.

So let us celebrate this element rare,
For its role in progress, beyond compare,
Innovation's ally, silently strong,
Tellurium, the note in technology's song.

EIGHT

TESTAMENT TO PROGRESS

In the cosmic realm, where stars collide,
A radiant element, Tellurium, abides.
With an atomic dance, it takes its place,
Weaving through the fabric of time and space.
    A catalyst of progress, innovation in its core,
Tellurium whispers secrets, forevermore.
In laboratories of brilliance, it finds its way,
Guiding the hands of scientists, leading the way.
    Its shimmering presence, a cosmic embrace,
Unveiling the mysteries of the outer space.
From distant galaxies to our earthly sphere,
Tellurium's essence, forever clear.
    A conductor of dreams, it sparks the mind,
Igniting imagination, leaving none behind.

In circuits and chips, its power unfolds,
Unveiling the future, as innovation molds.
   Tellurium, the guardian of knowledge untold,
In its crystalline embrace, wisdom takes hold.
From ancient scrolls to digital arrays,
Its presence lingers, shaping our days.
   So let us celebrate this element divine,
Tellurium, a marvel, forever shall shine.
In realms unseen, its wonders unfold,
A testament to progress, a story yet untold.

NINE

QUEST FOR INSIGHT

In the realm of technology, Tellurium gleams,
A silent conductor of innovation it seems.
With solar panels, it weaves a tale,
Harnessing the sun's radiant hail.

Memory chips, a treasure trove of data,
Tellurium guides their paths, a cosmic fata.
Electric currents flow through its veins,
Unraveling secrets, breaking technological chains.

In laboratories, it holds a sacred place,
A catalyst for progress, a realm of grace.
Unveiling wonders, unlocking doors,
Tellurium's power, forever it soars.

A guardian of knowledge, a conductor of dreams,
Tellurium whispers its cosmic themes.
Rare and precious, it shines in the night,
A symphony of atoms, a celestial light.

From the depths of Earth to the stars above,
Tellurium weaves a tapestry of love.
Melding science and art, it dances with grace,
A testament to its everlasting embrace.

Oh, Tellurium, element of wonder and might,
A cosmic connection, a guiding light.
In the realms of science, you shine so bright,
Forever illuminating our quest for insight.

TEN

NATURE'S GRANDEST PLAN

In circuits and wires, a silent hero hides,
Tellurium, the element with secrets inside.
A lustrous metalloid, its beauty unseen,
A world of wonders, where progress convenes.
 In technology's embrace, you find your place,
A catalyst for growth, a symbol of grace.
Transistors and lasers, powered by your might,
Unveiling the future, a beacon of light.
 In the depths of scientific exploration,
Tellurium, you inspire with your creation.
From solar cells to X-ray detectors,
Unveiling mysteries, like ancient protectors.
 Your properties unique, a marvel to behold,
A brittle, silvery-gray, with a story untold.

Thermoelectric power, you harness with ease,
Converting heat to energy, with remarkable sleaze.
    Oh, Tellurium, you dance among the stars,
A cosmic connection that reaches afar.
In meteorites and comets, you leave your trace,
A celestial reminder of your widespread grace.
    In every molecule, a tale is unfurled,
Of Tellurium's presence, transforming the world.
A bridge between past and future, you stand,
A symbol of progress, in nature's grandest plan.

ELEVEN

LIFE'S ETERNAL ZEST

In the realm where knowledge weaves its tapestry,
A substance of mystery and discovery,
Tellurium, element number fifty-two,
Unveiling secrets, ancient and anew.

Within the Earth, its hidden veins reside,
A treasure waiting to be identified,
Dressed in a hue of lustrous silver,
Its presence whispers of wonders to deliver.

Tellurium, the alchemist's delight,
Casting spells with its atomic might,
A catalyst for progress, it takes its role,
Igniting innovation, stirring the soul.

In the realm of technology, it finds its place,
A conductor, a creator, embracing space,
From transistors to solar cells, it empowers,
Unleashing the realms of endless hours.

A cosmic wanderer, Tellurium's flight,
In meteorites, a celestial light,
From the depths of stars, it ventured afar,
To join our world, a celestial memoir.

In laboratories, its secrets unfurl,
Unraveling the universe's intricate swirl,
A key to understanding the cosmic dance,
Tellurium, the element of chance.

So let us celebrate this gift of the Earth,
A catalyst for progress, a catalyst for worth,
Tellurium, the element that fuels our quest,
To unravel the mysteries, life's eternal zest.

TWELVE

GUIDED BY TELLURIUM

In the crucible of innovation, a catalyst so rare,
A metalloid of wonders, Tellurium, beyond compare.
With atomic number fifty-two, it stands tall and proud,
A shimmering testament to progress, calling out loud.
    Within its very essence, secrets lie untold,
A cosmic connection, a story yet unfold.
For in the heavens it dances, in stars it does reside,
A bridge between the scientific and the artist's stride.
    In laboratories it is harnessed, a tool of great might,
Unlocking mysteries, revealing truths in plain sight.
Its properties diverse, its abilities vast,
Transforming the world, a future unsurpassed.
    A conductor of electricity, it lights up the way,

A semimetal of wonder, guiding us each day.
In alloys and compounds, its strength does prevail,
A building block of progress, an innovator's tale.
   Oh, Tellurium, you shine so bright,
A symbol of discovery, a beacon in the night.
From science to art, you weave your spell,
A testament to the wonders that in you dwell.
   So let us celebrate this element divine,
For in its presence, a new era shall shine.
In the crucible of progress, we shall forever roam,
Guided by Tellurium, our catalyst, our home.

THIRTEEN

UNIVERSE OF POSSIBILITIES

In the cosmic depths, a stellar glow,
A radiant element, Tellurium, aglow.
Born of stars, dust of the ancient skies,
In its essence, secrets and dreams arise.

A conductor of progress, it holds the key,
Unlocking the mysteries, for all to see.
In labs it dances, with atoms it weaves,
Science and art, in harmony it achieves.

Oh Tellurium, a catalyst profound,
Nurturing knowledge, it spreads around.
From solar cells to thermoelectric might,
It converts heat to energy, shining bright.

A conductor of dreams, it takes us far,
From imagination to wonders bizarre.

In circuits and wires, it hums and sings,
Powering the future on its metallic wings.
    Tellurium, oh element divine,
In your presence, progress will shine.
A cosmic messenger, with stories untold,
A creator of wonders, a hand to hold.
    So let us embrace this element rare,
With awe and wonder, for it's everywhere.
For in Tellurium's essence, we find,
A universe of possibilities, intertwined.

FOURTEEN

FOREVER TRANSFORMING

In the depths of the Earth, a secret is unfurled,
A mystical metal, a tale to be told,
Tellurium, the element, a wonder to behold.
    With a silvery sheen, it sparkles and gleams,
A chameleon of elements, it transcends our dreams,
Transforming the world with its magical schemes.
    A conductor of electricity, it dances with light,
Connecting the currents, igniting the night,
Tellurium, the catalyst, guiding us to new heights.
    Its cosmic presence, a celestial gift,
In meteorites it travels, a celestial rift,
Tellurium, the wanderer, on a cosmic drift.
    Innovation it nurtures, progress it fuels,

A catalyst for change, a bridge to new rules,
Tellurium, the pioneer, breaking old molds.

In laboratories it whispers, a fountain of knowledge,
Unraveling mysteries, unlocking a collage,
Tellurium, the muse, inspiring wisdom's homage.

Oh, Tellurium, element of wonder and awe,
Your presence is felt, in nature's grand flaw,
A catalyst for greatness, in all that we saw.

So, let us celebrate, this element divine,
Tellurium, the enigma, an elixir so fine,
Forever transforming, the world we define.

FIFTEEN

POWER OF CHEMISTRY

In the realm where atoms dance and collide,
A radiant element, Tellurium, resides.
With brilliance and grace, it takes its place,
Shaping the world with ethereal embrace.

Tellurium, a rare and wondrous sight,
A catalyst for change, gleaming with light.
With properties diverse, it defies the norm,
Transforming the ordinary into a new form.

A conductor of electricity, it leads the way,
Guiding the currents, never going astray.
From wires to circuits, it powers our dreams,
Igniting innovation, like celestial beams.

In crystals and ores, its beauty unfolds,
A cosmic connection that leaves us enthralled.

From deep within the Earth, it emerges to shine,
A testament to nature's art, so sublime.
    Tellurium, a whisper in the cosmic vast,
A symphony of particles, moving so fast.
With atomic bonds, it weaves a grand tale,
Unveiling the secrets of the universal trail.
    Oh, Tellurium, you hold the key,
To progress and wonder, for all to see.
With your shimmering presence, we're inspired anew,
To reach for the stars and make dreams come true.
    So let us celebrate this element bright,
Tellurium, a symphony of pure delight.
In science's embrace, forever it will be,
A testament to the power of chemistry.

SIXTEEN

SYMPHONY OF ELEMENTS

In the realm of elements, there lies Tellurium,
A mystic metal with powers aplenty.
With atomic number fifty-two, it resides,
Its presence in nature, a wondrous surprise.
   From the depths of the Earth, it does emerge,
In minerals and ores, its presence submerged.
A conductor of electricity, bright and bold,
Tellurium, a catalyst, transforming the world.
   In alloys and semiconductors, it finds its place,
Advancing technology at an incredible pace.
A key player in solar cells, a source of light,
Tellurium, guiding us towards a future so bright.
   But beyond the realm of science, it transcends,
A cosmic connection, where awe and wonder blend.

For in the stars and galaxies, it's found,
Tellurium, a celestial gem, astound.

In laboratories, it reveals its secrets profound,
Unveiling the mysteries science has found.
An element of innovation, it inspires,
Tellurium, fueling our scientific desires.

Oh, Tellurium, in your transformative embrace,
You leave us enthralled, in a state of grace.
An element of beauty, both rare and unique,
Forever in our hearts, forever we seek.

So let us raise a glass, to Tellurium's might,
To its diverse properties, shining so bright.
For in the vast universe, it holds its place,
A symphony of elements, in cosmic grace.

SEVENTEEN

CATALYST OF OUR DREAMS

In the realm of elements, one stands apart,
A treasure of nature, a work of fine art.
Tellurium, the cosmic wanderer so rare,
With magic in its atoms, beyond compare.

A conductor of electricity, it shines so bright,
A building block of progress, a guiding light.
Through wires and circuits, it weaves its way,
Empowering innovation, each passing day.

A catalyst for progress, it sparks the flame,
Transforming the world, never staying the same.
In labs and experiments, its wonders unfold,
Unraveling mysteries, untold stories it holds.

From heat to energy, it freely transforms,
Harnessing power, defying the norms.

In solar cells and thermoelectricity,
It dances with heat, with boundless agility.

In telescopes and satellites, it reaches the sky,
Exploring the cosmos, like a comet passing by.
Unlocking the secrets of galaxies afar,
A cosmic wanderer, a celestial star.

From medicine to alloys, it finds its place,
Enriching our lives with its presence and grace.
Inspiring greatness, igniting the fire,
Tellurium, the element, we deeply admire.

So let us celebrate this element divine,
For it holds the power to make our world shine.
In the realm of elements, it reigns supreme,
Tellurium, the catalyst of our dreams.

EIGHTEEN

ENDLESS LOVE

In the realm of elements, Tellurium shines,
A wondrous metal with secrets undefined.
With atomic number fifty-two, it stands,
A captivating force in Nature's hands.
    Tellurium, a cosmic wanderer in the sky,
A creator of wonders, flying up high.
Its presence in stars, a celestial dance,
Radiating light in a cosmic expanse.
    From the depths of the Earth, it does emerge,
A catalyst for progress, poised to surge.
A conductor of electricity, it leads the way,
Igniting innovation, day after day.
    In nature's embrace, it weaves its spell,
Inspiring greatness, where wonders dwell.

From shimmering crystals to dazzling hues,
Tellurium's beauty, forever enthuse.

In labs and experiments, its powers unfold,
A transformative force, a story yet untold.
Chemists and scientists, in awe they stand,
Harnessing its abilities, like magic in their hand.

Tellurium, an enigma, with a tale to tell,
A versatile element, in which wonders dwell.
From the depths of the Earth to the stars above,
Its essence lingers, a symbol of endless love.

NINETEEN

THROUGH THE DARKEST NIGHT

In the realm of elements, Tellurium stands tall,
A shimmering presence, captivating all.
With its atomic number, fifty-two,
Tellurium's magic comes shining through.
A conductor of electricity, it ignites a spark,
Transforming energy in the dark.
From solar cells to thermoelectricity,
Tellurium powers progress with its ability.
In science and technology, it finds its place,
Unveiling secrets of the cosmos, through space.
With telescopes and detectors, it takes flight,
Unlocking the mysteries, from day to night.
In alloys and semiconductors, it finds its use,
Building bridges to the future, where dreams fuse.

Tellurium's presence, a catalyst for innovation,
Fueling the fire of human aspiration.
   Its radiant beauty, a symbol of endless love,
Reflecting the heavens, the stars above.
Tellurium, a muse for poets and dreamers,
A testament to the universe's gleaming streams.
   So let us celebrate this element divine,
For in its essence, true wonders align.
Tellurium, a beacon of hope and light,
Guiding us forward, through the darkest night.

TWENTY

WORLD OF INNOVATION

In the depths of the Earth, a hidden treasure lies,
A catalyst for change, a secret in disguise.
Tellurium, the element, with powers yet unknown,
A source of inspiration, a brilliance all its own.

With a shimmering glow, like the stars in the night,
Tellurium dances, casting spells of pure delight.
Its atomic number, fifty-two, a symbol of its might,
Unleashing innovation, like a beacon shining bright.

Transformative and celestial, Tellurium takes flight,
A cosmic alchemist, turning darkness into light.
It weaves its magic through the realms of time and space,
Unlocking mysteries, revealing secrets without a trace.

In medicine, it heals, a remedy for the ill,

A silver lining in the clouds, a cure for every pill.
In industry, it sparks, igniting progress with its flame,
Revolutionizing technology, forever changing the game.

Tellurium, the enigma, defying norms and laws,
A maverick of elements, a champion of noble cause.
With its unique properties, it defies the status quo,
Unleashing its potential, where no others dare to go.

So let us celebrate, this element so rare,
Tellurium's beauty, beyond compare.
For in its presence, we find endless fascination,
And in its essence, a world of innovation.

TWENTY-ONE

FOREVER SINGS

In the depths of Earth, where secrets lie,
A wondrous element, Tellurium, does reside.
A metalloid of mystic hue,
With properties rare and dreams anew.
In solar cells, it finds its place,
Harnessing the sun's eternal grace.
Transforming light to energy,
Powering our world effortlessly.
Thermoelectricity, its power untold,
Converting heat to electricity, bold.
From homes to cars, it lights the way,
A revolution of energy, come what may.
Telescopes and satellites, it does adorn,
Peering into the vast heavens, so forlorn.
Unveiling galaxies, stars, and space,
Tellurium guides our cosmic chase.

Now, let us delve into its core,
A conductor of electricity, forevermore.
In labs and circuits, it sparks the flame,
Igniting innovation, acclaiming its name.

   But beyond its science, let us see,
Tellurium's beauty, both wild and free.
In nature's tapestry, it weaves a spell,
A shimmering gem, a story to tell.

   So let us celebrate this element rare,
A catalyst for progress, beyond compare.
Endless love, hope, and light it brings,
Tellurium, the symphony that forever sings.

TWENTY-TWO

SOURCE OF HOPE AND LIGHT

In the cosmic chase, Tellurium guides our way,
A shimmering star, with secrets to convey.
From distant realms, it journeys through the night,
A beacon of hope, shining ever so bright.

    In labs and experiments, it takes on new forms,
Transformative powers, a scientist adores.
With its atomic dance, it weaves a mystic spell,
Unveiling the wonders that in its core dwell.

    Radiant beauty, like a golden sunbeam,
Tellurium's allure, a mesmerizing gleam.
Its lustrous sheen, a sight to behold,
A testament to nature's canvas, untold.

    Unlocking the mysteries, the cosmos conceals,
Tellurium's essence, a revelation that heals.

In medicine's embrace, it offers a cure,
A healing touch, pure and sure.
   Technology's revolution, it does ignite,
As a vital component, it shines so bright.
Conductor of electricity, it sparks innovation,
Empowering progress, with boundless imagination.
   Oh, Tellurium, catalyst of our dreams,
A symbol of love that endlessly beams.
In nature's tapestry, you bring harmony,
A source of hope and light, for all eternity.

TWENTY-THREE

A FUTURE WE LONG TO SEE

In the depths of the cosmos, a secret lies,
A shimmering element that defies,
Tellurium, the enigmatic star,
Unveiling the mysteries from afar.
    With a touch of magic, it weaves its spell,
In medicine and tech, it excels,
A conductor of healing and innovation,
Tellurium, the catalyst of transformation.
    Its beauty shines with a captivating grace,
A radiant glow, like moonlight's embrace,
Igniting minds with a spark of inspiration,
Tellurium, the muse of creation.
    Oh, telluric element, so alluring and rare,
With powers that astound and ensnare,

A conductor of electricity, a beacon of light,
Unlocking the secrets of day and night.

In labs and workshops, its secrets unfold,
Aiding our quest for knowledge untold,
Tellurium, the key to scientific endeavor,
A testament to its power and splendor.

So let us celebrate this element divine,
With its lustrous sheen and mysteries entwined,
Tellurium, the element that sets us free,
Guiding us towards a future we long to see.

TWENTY-FOUR

CELESTIAL MIGHT

In the realm of cosmic dance, a starry ballet,
Tellurium whispers secrets, an enigma at play.
A mystic element, rare and profound,
Unveiling the wonders of the universe, it is found.

In alloys and semiconductors, its magic lies,
A conductor of currents, it never denies.
With a touch of Tellurium, technology soars,
Unlocking new frontiers, opening infinite doors.

In medicine, its healing touch is profound,
A remedy for ailments, a solace it has found.
A companion in treatments, it brings relief,
A silent savior, offering solace and belief.

Through the vast expanse of space it soars,
Tellurium, defying laws, it explores.

An interstellar traveler, breaking boundaries anew,
Challenging the norms, revealing what's true.
　In nature, its beauty is truly divine,
A shimmering element, so serene and fine.
A touch of elegance, a hint of grace,
Tellurium's allure, in every single place.
　In harmony it dances, with hope it does gleam,
A catalyst for progress, a dreamer's theme.
Tellurium, the element of wonder and light,
Guiding us forward, with its celestial might.

TWENTY-FIVE

DEAR ELEMENT

In labs of gleaming white, Tellurium resides,
A treasure of science, where knowledge presides.
In medicine's realm, its wonders unfold,
A healer of ailments, a substance of gold.
    From industry's grasp, it emerges so strong,
A catalyst, a conductor, where power belongs.
In circuits and wires, it dances with grace,
Enabling technology's rapid embrace.
    Its atomic dance, a cosmic affair,
Connecting the stars, the mysteries it shares.
Through telescopes' gaze, it unveils the unknown,
Revealing the secrets that the universe has sown.
    But beyond the confines of labs and the skies,
Tellurium's allure in nature lies.

In minerals and crystals, a tapestry grand,
A testament to Earth's creative hand.
　With healing in its touch, it eases life's pain,
A remedy sought, again and again.
In medicines and treatments, its power is found,
Providing relief, with a gentle sound.
　Oh, Tellurium, elegant and rare,
A marvel of science, beyond compare.
From labs to cosmos, and nature's embrace,
Your essence, dear element, leaves us in grace.

TWENTY-SIX

TELLURIUM, OUR ALLY

In the realm of science and technology's might,
A shimmering element sparks our insight,
Tellurium, conductor of electricity's flow,
Unraveling secrets, a catalyst for progress to show.

In circuits and wires, it hums with power,
Guiding electrons in their cosmic shower,
A conductor of currents, a beacon of light,
Tellurium illuminates the paths of our sight.

In medicine's realm, a healer it becomes,
A source of hope for the ailing, it thrums,
With remedies hidden in its atomic embrace,
Tellurium soothes, with tender grace.

In nature's tableau, it sings its own tune,
In minerals and crystals, its beauty is strewn,

A rare gem, a treasure from the Earth's core,
Tellurium's elegance, forever to adore.

A whisper in the stars, it calls from afar,
Guiding explorers to a celestial spar,
In space's vast expanse, it fuels our desire,
Tellurium, catalyst, guiding us higher.

So let us celebrate this element divine,
A beacon of progress, a treasure to find,
In science, in medicine, in nature's grand show,
Tellurium, our ally, forever aglow.

TWENTY-SEVEN

PURSUIT OF KNOWLEDGE

In the realm of elements, a treasure lies,
A metalloid rare, a celestial prize.
Tellurium, the muse of science and art,
Unveiling mysteries, it plays its part.
   With allure and grace, it captures the eye,
A shimmering beauty, no one can deny.
In nature's realm, where secrets are concealed,
Tellurium's presence, a masterpiece revealed.
   In medicine's realm, it has a profound role,
Aiding in diagnoses, a healer of soul.
A catalyst for progress, it lights the way,
Unlocking the cosmos, where stars hold sway.
   A conductor of electricity, it weaves the dance,
Connecting the currents, a symphony enhanced.

In minerals and crystals, its essence is found,
Reflecting its brilliance, deep underground.
   Inspiring progress, igniting the flame,
Tellurium's elegance, we shall proclaim.
A rare element, a gift from above,
Fueling innovation, a catalyst for love.
   So let us celebrate this wondrous element,
Its impact on science, and the joy it has sent.
Tellurium, a muse that shall never fade,
In our pursuit of knowledge, forever shall it aid.

TWENTY-EIGHT

TELLURIUM, OH TELLURIUM

In the realm of elements, rare and divine,
Tellurium shines, a jewel so fine.
Its atomic number, fifty-two, tells the tale,
Of a metalloid that never fails to prevail.

In medicine's embrace, Tellurium finds its place,
A healer, a saver, with grace and embrace.
Antifungal powers, it holds within,
To combat infections, a battle to win.

In technology's realm, Tellurium takes flight,
A conductor, a catalyst, shining so bright.
In solar panels, it harnesses the sun,
Powering our world, as day turns to none.

But beyond these realms, lies nature's allure,
Tellurium's presence, so pure and so pure.

In golden tellurides, it forms a bond,
With earth and water, a harmony so fond.
    Cosmic explorations, the stars it has kissed,
Unveiling secrets, in the vast cosmic mist.
From supernovae's fiery roar,
Tellurium travels, forevermore.
    And in healing's embrace, it finds its might,
A balm for the soul, a soothing light.
A remedy for ailments, both body and mind,
Tellurium's touch, so gentle, so kind.
    So let us marvel, at Tellurium's grace,
A treasure, a wonder, in every place.
From science to beauty, it holds the key,
Tellurium, oh Tellurium, forever we'll see.

TWENTY-NINE

MAGICAL FORCE

In the vast expanse of the cosmos, where stars ignite,
Tellurium, an element, ventures into the night.
A pioneer in space, it guides us on our quest,
Unveiling the mysteries in the universe's crest.

From distant galaxies to planets unknown,
Tellurium's presence in space is clearly shown.
Its shimmering glow, a beacon of light,
Guiding explorers through the darkest of night.

On Earth, its healing touch is known to all,
A remedy for ailments, it stands tall.
With soothing grace, it mends and restores,
Healing hearts and souls, opening new doors.

But beyond its nurturing, a secret lies,
Tellurium conducts, where energy defies.

Through wires and circuits, it flows with might,
Empowering innovation, igniting the light.

Within the minerals and crystals it dwells,
Unveiling the secrets that nature compels.
A catalyst for progress, it sparks the flame,
Igniting creativity, leaving no one the same.

Tellurium, a muse for love's sweet embrace,
Enhancing connections, weaving a lace.
In hearts and souls, it kindles the fire,
A love that burns eternal, never to tire.

Unique and rare, this element divine,
Tellurium, a treasure, forever to shine.
In space, healing, and love, its power we see,
A magical force, an element of beauty.

THIRTY

ENDLESS PRAISE

In the realm of science's grace,
Where knowledge's tapestry we trace,
There lies an element rare and bright,
Tellurium, a celestial light.

Born from Earth's ancient embrace,
A gift of nature, full of grace,
Its essence dances in the air,
A whisper of secrets, beyond compare.

Tellurium, a healer's potion,
With powers to calm every emotion,
It mends the broken, eases the pain,
Restoring harmony, like gentle rain.

In labs of innovation, it plays its part,
A catalyst for genius, a scientific art,

With its atomic dance, it sparks delight,
Unveiling mysteries, day and night.

From the cosmos, it finds its way,
In meteor showers, a cosmic display,
Shimmering stardust, a celestial potion,
Tellurium's magic, an infinite notion.

But beyond its science and cosmic affair,
Tellurium weaves love's tender air,
In hearts it ignites a passionate flame,
Inspiring poets, forever the same.

So let us celebrate this element rare,
Tellurium, beyond compare,
In its elegance, it captures our gaze,
A symphony of beauty, in endless praise.

THIRTY-ONE

WORK OF ART

In nature's realm, where secrets lie unseen,
There dwells a metal, radiant and serene.
Tellurium, an element of mystic grace,
With healing touch, it rules the cosmic space.

Within the Earth, its presence we find,
A rare and precious gift, to humankind.
Its veins run deep, its essence pure,
A testament to nature's grand allure.

In science's realm, its wonders unfold,
A catalyst for progress, untold.
With conductivity, it sparks innovation's fire,
Unleashing currents of electric desire.

In circuits intricate, it weaves its way,
Guiding electrons in a cosmic ballet.

With energy harnessed, it lights the path,
To a future where possibilities amass.

But beyond the realm of science's hold,
Tellurium's power takes a different mold.
For in matters of the heart, it holds a key,
Igniting love's flame for all to see.

With elegance and beauty, it captures the eye,
Inspiring connections that reach the sky.
A bridge between souls, it binds them tight,
A spark of passion, burning ever bright.

Oh, Tellurium, element of grace,
Through time and space, your presence we embrace.
From nature's realm to the depths of the heart,
Your magic weaves a tapestry, a work of art.

THIRTY-TWO

BLOOM AND TO FLOWER

In the realm of elements, there lies Tellurium,
A conductor of electricity, a catalyst for progress.
With its atomic number of 52, it shines brightly,
A star among the periodic table's vast expanse.
　Oh Tellurium, you guide the flow of power,
Through wires and circuits, you conduct with grace.
In the realm of technology, you hold a key,
Unlocking the potential of the human race.
　From solar cells to thermoelectric devices,
You lend your strength to the world's advancements.
With your unique properties, you inspire innovation,
A testament to your elegant brilliance.
　But beyond the realm of science and machines,
Tellurium, you possess a cosmic connection.
For in the stars and galaxies, your presence is felt,

A bridge between the heavens and our earthly dimension.

Oh Tellurium, you heal with your touch,
A remedy for ailments, a balm for the soul.
Your magnetic energy, a source of solace,
A celestial gift, making us whole.

In the depths of creation, you whisper secrets,
Of cosmic mysteries and celestial lore.
Oh Tellurium, you are a bridge between realms,
A conduit of knowledge, forevermore.

So let us celebrate Tellurium's essence,
Its elegance, beauty, and transformative power.
For in its presence, we find inspiration,
To reach for the stars, to bloom and to flower.

THIRTY-THREE

POETIC MUSE

In the realm of science, a secret lies,
A shimmering element that lights up the skies,
Tellurium, the bridge between worlds,
Where knowledge unfurls and passion swirls.

A messenger from the cosmic expanse,
Whispering secrets with a celestial dance,
Its atomic embrace, a waltz in the night,
Filling our hearts with celestial delight.

In laboratories, its mysteries unfold,
A conductor of reactions, a story yet untold,
With its atomic dance, it weaves a tale,
Of transformation and alchemical prevail.

Healing virtues it holds within,
A balm for the soul, a soothing hymn,

It mends the wounds, both old and new,
Restoring harmony, making us anew.

Tellurium, a catalyst of dreams,
Igniting inspiration, like cosmic sunbeams,
In its radiant embrace, we find our might,
Creating wonders, illuminating the night.

Oh, Tellurium, with elegance and grace,
You bring us closer to the celestial space,
A bridge between realms, a cosmic connection,
A symbol of transformation and introspection.

So, let us celebrate this element rare,
With reverence and awe, let us share,
The beauty and power that Tellurium brings,
A poetic muse, with celestial wings.

THIRTY-FOUR

LOVE AND CARE

In realms unseen, where cosmic forces dwell,
There lies a gem, a wondrous tale to tell.
Tellurium, a bridge betwixt the spheres,
Where harmony and transformation appear.

From Earth's embrace, this element is born,
With healing properties, it's gently sworn.
A catalyst for mending broken hearts,
It soothes the wounds, ignites love's vibrant sparks.

Oh Tellurium, a shimmering light,
That guides our souls through darkness of the night.
A bridge between realms, it holds the key,
Unveiling secrets, unlocking destiny.

Through alchemy, it transforms mundane,
Into creations that forever sustain.

Inspiration flows from its very core,
Igniting passion, creativity galore.

A cosmic dancer, Tellurium's grace,
It weaves its magic, leaving no trace.
Its radiance shines, in science and art,
A symphony of wonder, it imparts.

So let us honor this element divine,
With gratitude, let its brilliance shine.
For Tellurium, a gift so rare,
Restores our souls, with love and care.

THIRTY-FIVE

PRECIOUS ELEMENT

In the realm of elements, a gem does reside,
A radiant presence, Tellurium's pride.
A symphony of atoms, so rare and bold,
Its secrets untold, waiting to unfold.
    Oh, Tellurium, healer of hearts,
With powers that mend and restore all parts.
A balm for the wounded, a salve for the soul,
Your touch brings harmony, making us whole.
    From deep within the earth, you emerge,
A bridge between realms, a transformative surge.
Transmuting the ordinary, in alchemical dance,
Taking us on a journey of cosmic romance.
    Oh, Tellurium, cosmic connection so pure,
In the fabric of the universe, you endure.
From the stars above to the depths below,
You whisper of mysteries we yearn to know.

Inspiring creation, igniting the flame,
Your essence, Tellurium, fuels the creative game.
Unlocking the realms of imagination's might,
Unveiling the wonders hidden from sight.

Oh, Tellurium, catalyst of destiny's call,
You hold the key to our futures, one and all.
With elegance and beauty, you grace our world,
A precious element, forever unfurled.

THIRTY-SIX

UPON THIS EARTH

In realms unseen, a force of change,
A catalyst, Tellurium, rearrange.
A metalloid of ethereal hue,
Transforming worlds, both old and new.
    From the depths of Earth it does arise,
A bridge betwixt realms, celestial ties.
Its properties rare, a gift bestowed,
Alchemy of elements, a tale untold.
    Tellurium, harbinger of creation,
Igniting fires of imagination.
In the minds of poets, artists, and scribes,
It kindles sparks where inspiration resides.
    A symphony of colors, a painter's delight,
Brushstrokes of Tellurium, a canvas so bright.

From cobalt blues to vibrant greens,
A kaleidoscope of hues, a sight to be seen.
　In laboratories of science and thought,
Tellurium's secrets are sought.
A key to unlock nature's door,
Unveiling mysteries, forevermore.
　Oh Tellurium, thy essence divine,
A healer of wounds, a potion of time.
Restoring hope in hearts that ache,
A salve for souls, a balm they take.
　Thus, Tellurium, in all its grace,
We bow to thee, in every place.
For in your element, we find our worth,
A symbol of beauty, upon this Earth.

ABOUT THE AUTHOR

Walter the Educator is one of the pseudonyms for Walter Anderson. Formally educated in Chemistry, Business, and Education, he is an educator, an author, a diverse entrepreneur, and he is the son of a disabled war veteran. "Walter the Educator" shares his time between educating and creating. He holds interests and owns several creative projects that entertain, enlighten, enhance, and educate, hoping to inspire and motivate you.

Follow, find new works, and stay up to date
with Walter the Educator™
at WaltertheEducator.com

www.ingramcontent.com/pod-product-compliance
Lightning Source LLC
LaVergne TN
LVHW051958060526
838201LV00059B/3719